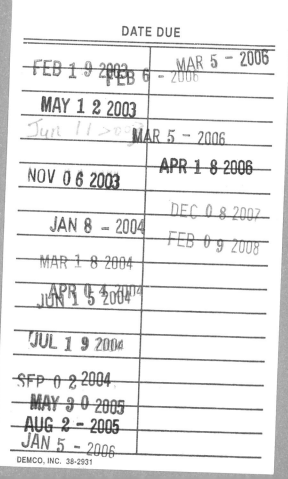

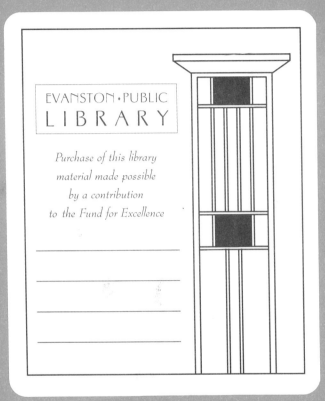

# DINOSAUR WORLD

# Bird-footed Dinosaurs

## Robin Birch

CHELSEA
CLUBHOUSE
An Imprint of Chelsea House Publishers
A Haights Cross Communications Company
Philadelphia

This edition first published in 2003 in the United States of America by Chelsea Clubhouse, a division of Chelsea House Publishers and a subsidiary of Haights Cross Communications.

Chelsea Clubhouse
1974 Sproul Road, Suite 400
Broomall, PA 19008-0914

The Chelsea House world wide web address is www.chelseahouse.com

Library of Congress Cataloging-in-Publication Data

Birch, Robin.
  Bird-footed dinosaurs / by Robin Birch.
  p. cm. — (Dinosaur world)

  Summary: Describes the appearance, eating habits, and habitat of bird-footed dinosaurs, including Iguanodon, Hypsilophodon, Maiasaura, Parasaurolophus, and Corythosaurus.

  Includes index.
  ISBN 0-7910-6989-3
  1. Ornithischia—Juvenile literature. [1. Ornithischians. 2. Dinosaurs.] I. Title. II.Series.
  QE862.O65 B57 2003
  567.914—dc21

                                                            2002000845

First published in 2002 by
MACMILLAN EDUCATION AUSTRALIA PTY LTD
627 Chapel Street, South Yarra, Australia, 3141

Copyright © Robin Birch 2002
Copyright in photographs © individual photographers as credited

Edited by Angelique Campbell-Muir
Illustrations by Nina Sanadze
Page layout by Nina Sanadze

Printed in China

**Acknowledgements**

Department of Library Services, American Museum of Natural History (neg. no. PK51), p. 9; Auscape/ James L. Amos & Peter Arnold, p. 5, Auscape/Parer & Parer-Cook, p. 13; © The Natural History Museum, London, pp. 8 (bottom), 12, 16; Getty Images/Photodisc, p. 24; Royal Tyrrell Museum of Palaeontology/ Alberta Community Development, pp. 8 (top), 29.

While every care has been taken to trace and acknowledge copyright, the publisher tenders their apologies for any accidental infringement where copyright has proved untraceable.

# Contents

# Dinosaurs

Dinosaurs lived and died millions of years ago.

After dinosaurs died, their bones sometimes became buried. We know what dinosaurs were like because scientists have dug up and studied their bones.

# Bird Feet

Some dinosaurs ate animals and others ate plants. Some of the plant-eating dinosaurs had feet like birds' feet. These dinosaurs had three toes on each back foot.

Bird-footed dinosaurs probably walked on both their arms and legs. But they probably ran fastest on just their legs.

The plant-eating, bird-footed dinosaurs had hard beaks. Usually they did not have teeth in their beaks. Instead, these dinosaurs had sharp teeth farther back in their cheeks. It is hard to see these teeth in their **skulls**.

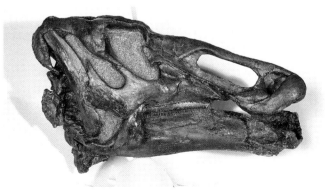

Bird-footed dinosaurs laid eggs, as all other dinosaurs did. Some eggs did not hatch. After many years, they turned into rock. The rock eggs are a type of **fossil**.

# Iguanodon

(ih-GWAN-uh-don)

Iguanodon was a big, heavy dinosaur. It had strong back feet with three toes on each foot. It also had a long, **stiff** tail.

Instead of thumbs on its front hands, Iguanodon had strong, sharp spikes made of bone. Iguanodon may have used these spikes to fight other dinosaurs if it was attacked.

Iguanodon probably bit off ferns and other low plants with its beak. Then it chewed them with its cheek teeth.

Iguanodon teeth

Iguanodons lived in large groups called **herds**. The herds usually roamed flat lands near rivers in search of food. Today, many animals live in herds.

13

# Hypsilophodon

(hip-sil-OFF-o-don)

Hypsilophodon was a small, slim dinosaur. It could probably see very well with its large eyes.

Hypsilophodon could run very fast on its long legs. It held its stiff tail out to run. The tail helped the dinosaur keep its balance.

Hypsilophodon had teeth in the top of its hard beak, which it used to grab and tear plants. It also had cutting teeth in its cheeks. Bones dug up from the ground show us how Hypsilophodon looked.

Hypsilophodon lived in flat meadows near rivers and lakes. It lived in herds, which gave it some protection from **predator** dinosaurs.

# Maiasaura

(mah-ee-ah-SAWR-uh)

Maiasaura was a large dinosaur. Its hard beak was like a duck's bill. Maiasaura is called a duck-billed dinosaur.

Maiasaura had long arms and a stiff tail. It had small bumps called **crests** in front of its eyes.

Maiasaura herds lived on **plains** by the sea. They used dirt and mud to build nests. The females laid about 20 eggs in each nest. When the eggs hatched, the young dinosaurs stayed in their nests.

Maiasaura looked after its young in the nest. Parents fed their young and protected them from other dinosaurs. Young Maiasauras left the nest when they were bigger.

# Parasaurolophus

(par-ah-SAWR-OL-uh-fus)

Parasaurolophus was a large, duck-billed dinosaur. The lower beak of the dinosaur's bill was shorter than the upper beak. Parasaurolophus used its beak to break off leaves to eat.

Parasaurolophus probably walked on four legs most of the time. It had a long crest on its head.

The dinosaur's crest had a long **hollow** tube inside it. Parasaurolophus probably used the crest to make hooting sounds. The crest would have worked like a musical instrument.

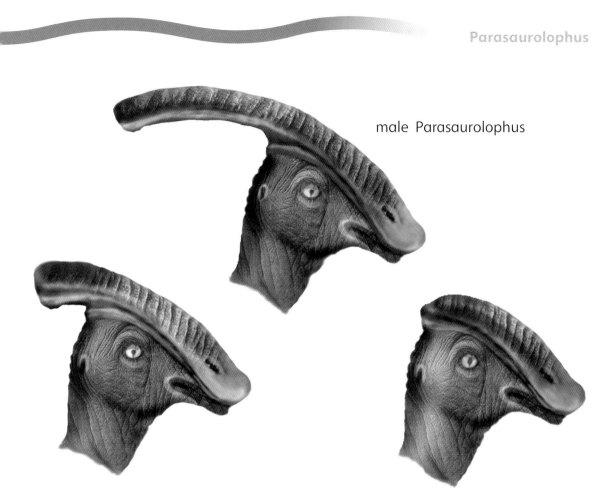

male Parasaurolophus

female Parasaurolophus

young Parasaurolophus

Members of Parasaurolophus families had different crests. Each kind of crest made its own sounds. Adult males had the longest crests.

# Corythosaurus

(ko-RITH-uh-SAWR-uhs)

Corythosaurus was a duck-billed dinosaur. It had a large, rounded crest made of bone on top of its head.

Corythosaurus had no teeth in its beak. But it had many cheek teeth for grinding leaves to eat. It had a bent neck and a straight tail.

Corythosaurus had hollow tubes inside its large crest. The tubes helped the dinosaur make loud hooting sounds. The male's crest may have changed color when it was ready to mate with a female.

Corythosaurus lived on plains near the sea. Scientists have dug up its bones, which show that Corythosaurus was about 21 feet (6 meters) tall and 30 feet (9 meters) long.

# Names and Their Meanings

"Dinosaur" means "terrible lizard."

"Iguanodon" means "**iguana** tooth."

"Hypsilophodon" means "high-**ridge** tooth."

"Maiasaura" means "good mother lizard."

"Parasaurolophus" means "similar crested lizard."

"Corythosaurus" means "**helmet** lizard."

# Glossary

**crest**       a ridge on an animal's body; scientists think some crests gave dinosaurs a better sense of smell or helped them make sounds.

**fossil**       something left behind by a plant or animal that has been preserved in the earth; examples are dinosaur bones and footprints.

**helmet**       a hard covering that protects the head

**herd**       a large group of animals that live together

**hollow**       to be empty inside

**iguana**       a type of lizard that lives today

**plain**       a large area of land that is mainly flat

**predator**       an animal that hunts other animals for food

**ridge**       a long raised area

**skull**       the bones of the head

**stiff**       does not bend

# Index